i'm not thousandfurs

sarah menefee

curbstone press

1986 © Sarah Menefee
ALL RIGHTS RESERVED

printed in the U.S.
by Curbstone Press
typeset by YOUR TYPE

LC: 85-48297
ISBN: 0-915306-59-X

This book was supported in part by
The National Endowment for the Arts,
and The Connecticut Commission on the
Arts, a State agency, whose funds
are recommended by the Governor and
appropriated by the State Legislature

distributed by
The Talman Company, Inc.
150 Fifth Avenue, Room 514
New York, NY 10011

published by
CURBSTONE PRESS
321 Jackson Street
Willimantic, CT 06226

contents

we revere him Bobby Sands in *37*
tears in our hearts which make us human *38*
the day the Blue Angels screamed overhead *39*
today from Greensboro to Greenham Common *40*
a woman serves somebody else's food and stands by *41*
we don't care we do ok *42*
the blood of Colorado miners *43*
little donkey tethered outside the Mark Hopkins *44*
you northamerican poets *45*
a billboard for Egg McMuffin seen from the bus on Mission *46*
all evening writing *47*
neutral and ironic Naipaul is better *48*
I feel afraid that I don't feel before *49*
poor Mexico *50*
another also alien in a meat- *51*
the price on the head of a cut rose *52*
people seem to be in such nasty moods lately *53*
the family of Eugene Barnes *54*
a man with a backpack on and a windy face *55*
a propos some trivial condescending *56*
we know him as the gum-sticker *57*
two boys in their early teens *58*
it's the world of the scavenger *59*
washing potatoes at the sink I think *60*
with a splintery stick of wood *61*

i'm not
thousandfurs

outside it was raining
outside the aluminum-sided trailer
outside the urns and hedges of the miniature golf
course and the shoulder and the gully
full of blooming mustard

by the porch of the crippled furnace cleaner
my mother knew the yellow roses bloom
late May for about two weeks in the alley
through the chain link fence on the way
to the liquor store toward evening
for a can of ravioli and a newspaper
with Zaire in the headlines

I saw her walk by the hotel
she put her hand up to her hairdo
she was wearing lavender pants
something caught my eye about the way
she put her hand up to her helmet of hair
when the wind came up blowing the fog
over the sun I thought she's hurrying home
to a piece of meat thawed out in the sink
to peel potatoes and since it's Wednesday
watch Charlie's Angels and Vega$
and later the Tonight Show the way we used to

they were very paranoid about smoking grass
in the parked truck up the canyon
where the water master lived
below the Mountain View Cemetery
they kept imagining red lights and sirens
so they went back to the apartment
to have a threesome with fat Bill who was half blind
and had black stinking pigmud under his balls

then I was in the Little Brown Jug
which was supposed to be a pickup bar
he said he'd lost those front teeth in Nam
he must have been a Paiute his face shone
not the young one who followed me into the cab
that was years later up north of town
but 1968 the Year of the Monkey posters
in the Horseshoe Club for the busloads
of keno players from Chinatown

we drove up north of town past the city dump
looked at the lights below and the starry sky
he asked me if I believed in UFO's
no I don't think there's anything up there
we looked out at the arc of the Milky Way
I thought about the night I came up here
two years before with Bill the orderly
he put his finger in me as he drove
parked up here by the gravel pit and fucked
in the back seat then he fell asleep
I cried a little in loneliness and looked
at the clustered stars and the lights of town
a year later those stars shot down
rays of pain to burn me alive
in agony my body gave off the smell
of roses half of California with me inside
the peeling stucco walls of Camarillo
in the rusty autumn hills my breasts weeping
a clear fluid from all the Thorazine
a mynah bird in the men's ward wolf-whistled
when I swung on the swings on the grounds
back and forth safe in the rocky hills
making beds in the wards talking to the old
black homeless woman who knew anecdotes
about all the presidents the word salad woman
tomato tomato the boy of twelve walking
on the path saying in a singsong the atoms
make the molecules the molecules make
the elements the elements make the bodies
the bodies make the planets the planets make
the suns the suns make the galaxies the galaxies
make the universe the universes make the body of God

yes I remember that place he said when
we were hungry and there alone and he was
gone and no money and you pulled out a drawer
and there was a can of sardines oh I don't remember that
you and him went walking downtown and down
to the river to watch the pelicans dive
I was working in that dive dancing to get
dollars they felt where they put them in the dark
what was his name the dwarf when he came in
sad and mean he fell in love with each new one

she was thirty a busty redhead with two children
divorced too he'd been crazy and sometimes beat her
all winter depressed and on tranquilizers
we worked together as shills at the Primadonna
got off shift one night went over to the Palace Club
she and I together for a drink
there was Old King Cole with his pipe and bowl
jolly behind the bar on the napkins too
the row of bulbs that ran on a neon track
second gin and tonic Frank not really his friend
we went together he took me home that night
clung to him in the cell of his motel room
in the Irisher's by the river out west of town
for several weeks together all the time
eating take-out chicken on his tv tray
forty-two with silvery hair and sad sad pouches
under his eyes New York Irish his parents died
a Jewish man he called uncle took him in
lived over his deli the boys would swim
in the East River dove in naked carried
along caught on to some pier just before
they bobbed tender pale flotsam out to sea
his uncle died soon after even his dog died
we went to the movies Sam Peckinpah's
Straw Dogs and the other with Bob Dylan
riding after wild turkeys whipping with a bolo
their beautiful red wattled heads off
as they flap squawking in terror down a hill

every time I dream of you now
you've passed out drunk and I'm afraid
you stood in your only-son short pants
at the edge of the desert in the schoolyard
your memory but I see it
you and Stanley are ex-Marines
Stanley gives us three red plastic drink tokes
and we're there for the duration
we're there for three years
but when we sleep together
you weave the river willows
into a switchy hut above our heads
down on the bank of the Truckee River

this year I'll steal all my Christmas presents said
the big Jim Backus bartender they want these computer
games and digital watches his little twin
daughters smiling from a button on his red vest all
the off-shift employees sat drinking chartreuse
on a row of stools while the last leaves plastered
themselves to an alley where somebody wept
and a storm in its tall granite-gray tower
toppled above the mountains this day I've peeled
from between my breasts a heart-shaped and yellow
poplar leaf leaving a sadness as raw as the autumn mud

they put the gorilla in overalls said Spider
and set it out front clipping the bushes
and along comes a brother and says hey bro
they don't watch out another Abraham
Lincoln's gonna come along and free you
and he stepped around the pool table for his
shot complaining about his corns and laughing
his namesake medallion tarantula in plastic
against the smooth brown-black of his chest
fine homely face lit up how he moved that
moment I'll never not see his feet in their sandals

new moon over Oakland
children play down a steet of warehouses
grimy string mop over the gray porch rails
near a bush of roses wild and deep red-black
beautiful billboard couples in formal evening wear
elegantly raise together snifters of Korbel
over the brightly-lit Arco Service Center

not him standing on Market
under the low sky
talking about the FBI
gold teeth and lovecurl wig
no my face won't trade places with his
the way it does sometimes
or the ones behind me
the older guy saying to the teenage boy
I read somewhere that you could save $
sharing an apartment
look at the way he just wants attention
he's probably on SSI
got nothing to do all day
speaks with a southern accent
I never saw shoes like that
no I'm not worried about employment
or clothes that wear out
I'm not Thousandfurs
sleeping against a chain link fence
curled up under her coat of patchwork fur
her luggage at her feet
if I put fifty cents in a blind man's cup
while his german shepherd sleeps curled at his feet in a vest
maybe my face won't be his in a place of darkness
and soon the sun will break out for all of us

she took it out and smelled it a vial of oil
old woman in front three sisters got on chattering
all beautiful and fat saying I can smell roses what
your hair's coming out you're growing it on your chin
look good with moustache ha ha on my nose
pigs is the only things with hair on they nose
look at his legs he got some hair
wish I could whistle girl I never could

the morning we burned the mattress
we woke choking and dragged it out the back
pouring kettles of water into the smouldering hole
of blackened hay horsehair and cotton batting
you cut the burning mess out with a kitchen knife
then we mopped up and went back to sleep on the couch
I'm going to sleep all day I said and dreamed
I was riding a tricycle fast and euphorically on city streets
going to meet friends somewhere then return
through a filipino restaurant
where I score a large pickled or fermented fish
I eat as I walk along
taking out the long pointed bones

the radio woke me down below playing
kiss an angel good morning
a pickup truck parked below a camper
with a rustic shingled roof
a kid of three or so dandelion head
jumping on the sidewalk voice piping
goddamit I said walking into the bathroom
then the music stopped they drove away
and I missed the noise I wanted to look out
again and see where they were from
the way I wanted to remember about
the plump woman in the hamburger joint
a stark place like a doggie diner where
all the loose homeless souls were gathered
while a hard rain fell outside
and filled up all the valleys and hollows
we waited a while to get in and by the time
she opened we were soaked and shivering
and this cinderblock shelter lit by fluorescent lights
was as much a destination as we could dream of
because she was there a brown woman young
and short beautiful as the dirt I asked her
for tea as she went by a jumble of things
balanced on her tray she handed me a mug
and a tea bag with the words 'twig tea' printed
on it and said that's what you need to drink
to get warm before you go outside again

all over the world suddenly money
has lost its value except for one coin
the Greek nickel and what in the world is that
I told him my dream he said a month ago
I saw missiles falling on a park in San Francisco
coming down like rain I told you son
go out and buy a rifle from now on
we're going to have to live on what you shoot
small rabbits and birds that multiply
in the no-man's land between the lanes
of the freeway in the thickets of willow
and oleander there by the dead rivers
of abandoned cars rusting and silent

naked on the bed as it got dark
talking about the Christ
his long legs crossed under him
last night he was abusing some poor mis-
shapen creature a half-animal
Quasimodo then found himself
in army ranks holding an M-I rifle
maybe the cross-eyed man who came to me
last night to fuck me with his gun
it was his fair body Don Knotts had
when he came into the room followed by
the Egyptian eater of souls its low-
slung hippo rear cheetah torso and
heart-devouring crocodile maw

he sleeps at the edge of the side-
walk on the dusty strip stitched
by a few tough grass-runners out-
side the Social Services Department
weathered hand over eyes shut in ex-
hausted sleep a bit of midriff
bloated and red exposed to the care-
less traffic's looks half in the shadow
of the freeway overpass deep blank
dreams sinking him into the flanks
of the earth she smells of compassion
forever lost while a state employee
on her break drinking a Diet
Pepsi hurries back to work

before coffee on 9th and Mission
squinting into the balmy sunlight
he points to my leg saying
something I can't understand
chubby and brown he's about fifteen
wearing a crocheted hat of robin's-
egg blue and red like Curtis's hat
Curtis who died nine years ago
I look down and see on the thigh
of my jeans a white down feather
pick it off and shake it from my hand
mumbling pigeons it doesn't
want to go the breeze takes it up
around the corner and out of sight
next day I see him from the bus
at Civic Center can't mistake that hat

when the fog rolls in and the sun sets into the Pacific
out beyond the avenues and the zoo I feel sad
the way I used to for the tigers cold in their bleak cages
thinking about the Cambodian mountain people
how they creep into Golden Gate Park at night
to hunt squirrels and pigeons

night we've locked up the store and walking home
after ten-thirty past the theater a youngish man
in a dark suit black umbrella held over his head
against the rain is crouching over the curbside bags
outside of Colonel Sanders he's found a paper basket
of french fries still steaming and warm we
smell them as we walk home in our leaky boots

cop's horse seen from your window above
Columbus after two-thirty between
the cars of citizens honking
Mayakovsky's 'common animal
sorrow' the beaver and dildo
liquor store closed no vodka to-
night we'll send our hearts
on sparrow wings out over
the stunned young merrymaking
crowds to sip the temperate air
this first night of the year

Made in USA stencilled on a gun held
in the young hand of a peasant turned soldier
election day in El Salvador
a woman whose mouth has been shot out
by a government soldier trained in the Georgia woods
while walking to market to buy corn for her family's tortillas
a woman with five children whose husband has disappeared
a woman with a red hole where her mouth should be
whose silent scream of horror and pain
must make the earth itself shudder and lurch
on this day in March election day in El Salvador

this nameless old man herded to the polls
in his campesino straw hat back bent with a life-
time under the sun in the oligarchs' fields
just put an x by any name the one of your choice
says the paunchy goon in shades it doesn't matter
any way he chooses the same murderous terror
and he's no fool how well he knows it
moving his gnarled hand to a place away from any name
he draws a crooked x that's infinitely eloquent

look it's like the late late show
golden flares and beautiful explosions
look a father running his child's small arm dangling
down limp over and over the same scene playing
on the tv ignored supper in the oven
our boys young and beefy from small southern towns
run up the beaches in full war regalia
their faces pale as the expensive veal
served in Washington to visiting dictators

we revere him Bobby Sands in
our country all our brothers die
is bad your government helps them
killing women and children woman
with belly out like this with baby
shot his own flat belly scarred and near
the hairline lovely curly black usted
es lindo no lindo you say hermoso
I'm Maya you know the Popul Vuh
verdad es muy alta ah the Popul Vuh
de que pais cuantos anos tiene
your tongue in my mouth dulce oh sweet
I was engineer in my country

in memory: Jonestown

tears in our hearts which make us human
we call to you five years after nine hundred
lay together in final sleep
poor and forgotten their lives stolen
in cheap bright clothes arms thrown
around each other these gentle embraces
last futile comfort for the unwanted
gone somewhere we can't begin to imagine

our tears can't help now but we'd better cry them

the day the Blue Angels screamed overhead
on maneuver people stood on the corners
of San Francisco looking up at the sky
standing still and not really talking
watching these Ghost Dances of their nation
a storm of metal high above the city
above the Vietnamese children the garlic-
sellers in the Mission who dropped to the pavement
heads tucked into frail arms' protection

today from Greensboro to Greenham Common
old rites of spring preparations for Easter
daffodils stuck in a chain link fence in the shadow
of a windowless NATO defense bunker
while on this side of the Atlantic
in the land of the free home of the New Adam
again it's made clear the lynch law still rules
through an obscene marriage of white sheet and swastika
where vigilantes can gun down in daylight streets
any who oppose them and be acquitted today five years later
by a jury of their peers because those they shot were not human
but Communists though there they lay dying in pools of human
blood

a woman serves somebody else's food and stands by
while they eat her own children sit up hungry late
irons nice and flat the ruffles on somebody's clothes
you didn't see her she was the color of the shadow she waited in
she came in the back door early in the morning
back in the honeysuckle days of your nostalgia
she was young and pretty and had gold teeth
on hands and knees she scrubbed your floors with a brush
now she sweeps trash from the corners of your streets
with a broom and a workfare vest

we don't care we do ok
we're sure not communists anyway
or old or hungry with the rotten luck
to live in some nowhere place like Cleveland
we don't know what a harsh winter is
so if somebody on a tiny pension and half-
blind his gas cut off by the utility company
ninety years old burned up last February
trying to heat his room with a kerosene space
heater so what there's no guarantees in life
and anyway political poetry's so crude and boring

the blood of Colorado miners
machinegunned down by Rockefeller's cops in 1914
forms abstract expressionist smears on canvasses hung
on the boardroom walls of Chase Manhattan Bank

little donkey tethered outside the Mark Hopkins
for the amusement of the Democratic delegates
was about to foal and had to be taken away
a suffering living thing forced to play a cartoon
and the delegates went from bus to convention hall
to bus to hotel without accomplishing
anything or seeing anything new at all

you northamerican poets
masters of ennui-in-the-face-of-armageddon
welcome to the South African township of New Brighton
for the black workers of Port Elizabeth
a pile of rags by a dirt lot strewn with garbage
under a merciless streetlight near a row of scrapmetal huts
it's the body of a teenage boy shot through the chest
for singing walking in his brother's funeral procession
now tell the people here about your stalled aesthetics
your government grant your shattered linguistics
in the glare of Soweto and Sharpeville

a billboard for Egg McMuffin seen from the bus on Mission
said Rise and Die corporate death burgers a week or so before
the massacre in San Ysidro that night a young Salvadorean
spoke of his mother and brother dead his eyes blasted
with horror a stupor of liquor and uncried tears
the eye of a steer that once met mine through an airhole in
a dung-spattered cattle truck that passed my bus on Highway 80
an eye that sent straight to my brown mammal eye intelligent light
you said those newspaper photos look like any day in El Salvador
scoop up the bodies and call the bulldozers in
no he wasn't a veteran of Vietnam

all evening writing
pretty pieces of starsandmoon nostalgia
when what I begin to see
is that beauty doesn't exist in the fetish
of memory oh my youth my life
when what posseses me now is a vision
of a long broomstick the kind used for sweeping
hospital halls and military barracks
up the dead ass of Jeane Kirkpatrick

neutral and ironic Naipaul is better
on atmosphere and the petty human
aspirations of those in the struggle
the comic colonial aping of the western
centers of power and their costly sophistications
the populists and the ideologues equally laughable
Ghandi in England hanging out with the vegetarians
tongue-tied young barrister kicked off a South African train
it could have made a rather funny novel
but not his own version that dry self-serious
'experiment in truth' twenty years down there
and not one description of the landscape

I feel afraid that I don't feel before
says the Nicaraguan teacher speaking for us
here too trapped inside the beast
the big bootheel poised above their heads
coffee harvesters forced to take up arms
we are terrified too a terrible deja vu
as a statue of three Vietnam soldiers
goes up in Washington as the Rangers
and Green Berets get back into action

poor Mexico
upon the pyre of dependency
on oil an old curse disguised as a blessing
three hundred burned dead ten thousand homeless
already doomed in their poor workers quarters
poor Mexico
on the anniversary of your revolution
a turkey with singed feathers stands in the smoking rubble
half-alive cousin of those millions
eaten in thanks this week north of the border

another also alien in a meat-
packing plant cuts carcasses hanging from hooks
cattle skinned and quartered whole disembowelled hogs
ticket to this hall of opportunity
the magic green card reward four bucks an hour

the price on the head of a cut rose
given a million-fold on Valentines Day
is that of the view from a condominium
onto the hovels of the pickers of roses
who can't afford the rents in San Diego County
but find what they can to put together a shelter
cardboard and plastic bags thrown away
by the beauty-loving condominium dwellers
who didn't pay big money to be inflicted
with these eyesores right across the highway
and whose complaints as local taxpayers
are promptly answered by the Health Department
who put the dirty trash-heaps to the torch
and call the INS on the burnt-out families

people seem to be in such nasty moods lately
of course they are they feel the fascist squeeze
nobody wants to turn his back while his brother dies
at night a man walks by a bloated figure
huddled in the niche of an automatic versateller
and looks away his heart constricting
a black bilge of impotence in his guts
his body cries out to make some tender gesture

the family of Eugene Barnes
weeps beside his grave
their tears fall into the void
left by the life he couln't afford to live
in his temple a wound
out of which humanity's blood is oozing
in a series of institutional anterooms
not chosen as an emblem of compassion
like poor Baby Fae with her baboon's heart
listening to her mother's voice leak from a telephone

a man with a backpack on and a windy face
approaches me saying a quarter or a dime
or anything please I'm hungry
I lost my job and nobody wants me around
like a refrain to a poem I can't seem to write lately
all these faces of bewildered need
the cops on the corner exude an anxious black poisonous mist
and his wind-burned face hovers before my eyes
the coral red of his corderoy shirt

a propos some trivial condescending
remark I made to a man who pan-
handled this corner for a while
not bad-looking and not a looney
during those hot weeks when everyone
was complaining a plastic bottle of water
at his belt as he cashed in coins for a dollar bill
he retorted softly that he'd pleased a few woman
in his day I'd automatically seen him
sexless because he lived on the street
not punked-out but truly shabby
for some reason just now I thought of him

we know him as the gum-sticker
he doesn't come into the bookstore any more
he was caught sticking chewing gum between the pages of books
this large ungainly mongolian-looking man with one dead hand
held like an injured paw dragging a foot a bit
a black Elvis pompadour and worn black suit
the afternoon wind blowing the carbon from a charge
card form against his gimpy shoe did you see him last week
he went by with a not bad-looking woman
and a little doll of a girl can you imagine

two boys in their early teens
over a book of photos from Nicaragua
mira hey look man what's this the younger says
it's somebody burning his brother replies a human being
a blackened thing on a bed of ash in a village street
the words human being pronounced so clearly
that I shiver and in dream that night
restore the lines of tenderness the poem was missing
through endless nightmares of tortured Vietnam

it's the world of the scavenger
world from behind the cash register
causing rain on his meal at the corner can
as he comes in to browse through the store
out of the rain caused by his spittlefingers
wetting the earthy grapeleaves of Caravaggio
a scavenged red coat against the cold
and Pat with her handsome scowl at the door
they're making Hiroshima a joke
and ruling the world with my stolen womb

washing potatoes at the sink I think
about hunger and the cold night
smelling the fragrance of wet dirt on their skins
and imagine a baked potato hot
in a chapped hand out there in the night
pressed to the mouth of need like an earthy tit

with a splintery stick of wood
she pokes into Clown Alley trash bins
snagging aluminum cans to put in a big plastic bag
hello my dear you say her face lights up in a smile that's
infinitely human agespots dotted like freckles a straw hat
with a wide brim tied under her chin working this monster culture
salvaging something for money to eke out a meal in starving
Mozambique they squat in the parched dirt scrabbling
for grains of rice fallen from sacks we throw french fries
to the pigeons they strut and turn and peck at them
so they flip through the air the amber beads of their eyes
their coral feet oh grandmother all you toilers on this
earth we see you

235-235